the 29 th To...
Christmas, 1971

...atter and Alice and Char...

...ort Wayne fair they

made Doras dress over

r the 30 th cloudy

ent to Bluffton t...

them new dress Ad...

paper and a new

got done sowing s...

CLOTH & COMFORT

Pieces of Women's Lives from Their Quilts and Diaries

by RODERICK KIRACOFE

Photographs by SHARON RISEDORPH

CLARKSON POTTER/PUBLISHERS
NEW YORK

Excerpts came from original sources or were otherwise provided from: *Alabama Quilts,* copyright © 1981 Birmingham Museum of Art. *American Quilts: A Handmade Legacy,* copyright © 1981 The Oakland Museum. *The American Slave: A Composite Autobiography,* ed. by George P. Rawick, copyright © 1977 Greenwood Press, an imprint of Greenwood Publishing Group, Inc. Westport, Conn. Reprinted with permission. *Journey Into Childhood: The Autobiography of Lois Lenski,* copyright © 1972 Lois Lenski. J.B. Lippincott Company. Reprinted with permission of the Lois Lenski Covey Foundation. *Let Them Speak for Themselves: Women in the American West, 1849–1900,* ed. by Christiane Fischer, copyright © 1977 The Shoe String Press, Inc. *Miss Leslie's Lady's House-Book: A Manual of Domestic Economy* (18th edition, enlarged), Philadelphia: A. Hart, late Carey & Hart, 1853. The Western Reserve Historical Society, Cleveland, Ohio. *Old-Fashioned Quilts,* by Carlie Sexton, copyright © 1924 Register and Tribune Co., Des Moines. *Pieced by Mother: Over 100 Years of Quiltmaking Traditions,* Jeannette Lasansky, copyright © 1987 Oral Traditions Project. *Quilts: Their Story and How to Make Them,* Marie D. Webster, copyright © 1915, Doubleday, Page & Company. Used by permission. *Uncoverings 1981,* ed. by Sally Garoutte, copyright © 1982 American Quilt Study Group. *Universal Household Assistant or What Every One Should Know: A Cyclopedia of Practical Information,* gathered from the Most Reliable Sources, compiled and arranged by S. H. Burt, 1888, copyright © 1884 by A. L. Burt. *You May Plow Here: The Narrative of Sara Brooks,* copyright © 1986 Thordis Simonsen, W.W. Norton & Company, Inc., New York. Reprinted with permission.

Published by Clarkson N. Potter Inc., 201 East 50th Street, New York, New York 10022.
Member of the Crown Publishing Group.
Random House, Inc. New York, Toronto, London, Sydney, Auckland.
CLARKSON N. POTTER, POTTER, and colophon are trademarks of Clarkson N. Potter, Inc.

Manufactured in China
Design by MARGARET HINDERS

Library of Congress Cataloging-in-Publication Data
Kiracofe, Roderick.
Cloth & Comfort : pieces of women's lives from their quilts and diaries/ by Roderick Kiracofe;
photographs by Sharon Risedorph.—1st ed.
1. Women—United States—History—19th Century. 2. Quilting—United States—History—19th Century. 3. Quilts—United States—History—19th Century—Pictorial Works. 4. Material culture—United States —History—19th Century—Pictorial Works. 5. American diaries. I. Title II. Title: Cloth and Comfort.
HQ1418. K57 1994
305. 4' 0973' 09034—dc20   93-33816   CIP
ISBN 0-517-59795-0
10 9 8 7 6 5 4 3 2 1

First Edition

I dedicate this book to my mother,
Marjorie Pauling Kiracofe

acknowledgments

Ben Apfelbaum, Mary Barton, Doris Bassett, Gail Binney-Stiles, Helen Brubaker and Gratis (Ohio) Church of the Brethren, Gaby Burkert, Kris Cable, California Heritage Quilt Project, Robert Cargo, Ricky Clark, Alta and Charles Codding, Melba McBride Edwards, Charlotte Ekback, Mary Garry, Paul Gfroerer, Helen Gould, Catherine Grosfils, Joyce Gross, Donna and Bryce Hamilton, Patricia and Donald Herr, Ardis and Robert James, Marjorie and Eugene Kiracofe, Kate and Joel Kopp, Bibi Lamborn, Paula and Jim LeDuc, Eli Leon, Linda Lipsett, Living History Farms, Virginia McElroy, Sandra Mitchell, Roy R. Neuberger, The New England Quilt Museum, Rosalind Webster Perry, Louis Picek, Paul Pilgrim and Gerald Roy, Stella Rubin, Ellen Sampson, San Francisco Public Library, Jim Sheley, Merry Silber, Patricia Smith, Margaret Tennessen, Paul D. Yon and Bowling Green (Ohio) State University–Center for Archival Collections.

Special thanks to Debba Kunk Alexander, Peggy Arent, Jack B. Eiman, Penny McMorris, and Virginia Weaver.

Additional photographs by Geoffrey Clements (page 33), David Conklin (page 31), and Karen Steffens (page 59). Vintage photographs courtesy of the Ashland (Ohio) Historical Society (page 23), the Bowling Green (Ohio) State University–Center for Archival Collections (page 61), and The Western Reserve Historical Society, Cleveland (pages 41 and 53); all other vintage photographs are from the author's collection. *Woman with Sewing Box* (page 9) and *Lynchburg Negro Dance* (page 38) courtesy of Abby Aldrich Rockefeller Folk Art Center, Williamsburg, Virginia; portrait of Elizabeth and Mary Dagget (page 35) courtesy of the Connecticut Historical Society, Hartford, Connecticut; *The Quilting Bee* (page 13) courtesy of The Wisconsin Union Permanent Art Collection, The University of Wisconsin, Madison.

introduction

AS A BOY GROWING UP in northern Indiana, I remember going to local auctions to look through the household items and objects that people from earlier times had used in their daily lives. I liked the designs, the shapes, the colors and textures, and especially the fact that these objects were old.

I knew many of them were called "antiques," and that they had special monetary value to collectors. I even collected a few items myself, not because they were particularly valuable, but because I felt drawn to them and wanted to have these pieces of the past around me.

Strangely enough, I had never seen a quilt until I moved to Los Angeles in 1973. A friend had an appliquéd Butterfly quilt that her aunt in Wisconsin had made in the 1930s and had recently given to her. I was fascinated by the cloth her relative had chosen to cut and work with and was a bit envious of my friend for the good fortune of having a quilt made by someone she knew. In the summer of 1976, I moved to southern Ohio and once again indulged my passion for local auctions. One Saturday afternoon at a farmhouse auction, I approached a bed piled high with quilts. A floral basket appliquéd quilt caught my eye. As I examined the fabrics and studied the design, I became completely absorbed in thinking about who the maker might have been and what her thoughts were as she worked on it. I snapped out of my reveries just in time to be the highest bidder for this prize. Once it was mine, I wrapped it in my arms and carried it home.

In that same spirit, over the years I have collected "voices" from the past, bits and pieces of women's writing that capture in words the emotional resonance also conveyed by more tangible reminders of distant lives. As I researched my book *The American Quilt,* I came across stories, letters, inscriptions, household ledgers, and diary entries by the many women whose writings, along with their quilts, have remained intact. I found myself drawn to these fragments of lives because of the emotional responses they evoked in me.

These writings form a picture of women in the late nineteenth and early twentieth centuries sewing and filling up the minutes and hours of their days either as a part of their chores or after the "work" was done. Thousands of stitches marked the passing of the often-solitary homebound hours.

Inevitably, references to these hours of labor filled their records of daily life—"This is the last day of October and what a big days work I have done I comenced to sew at day light this morning and it is <u>most</u> sundown." These written remembrances, often anonymous and largely private thoughts, were rarely meant for anyone else to read. They are leftover pieces, patches of time that will never come again, threaded together with needlework memorabilia and details of quilts about which women wrote—and for which they felt justifiable, quiet pride.

In compiling these written fragments, I have often been struck by the realization that each individual life is itself a patchwork of experiences, both dramatic and mundane. Surprisingly, it is often the mundane rather than the dramatic that speaks to us across the years, linking the past to our own lives.

In diary entries made by Elizabeth Hosack Ayers in the late summer of 1865, numerous mentions of her quilting are threaded among the references to her upcoming twenty-fifth birthday and to letters exchanged between herself and her fiancé.

What isn't mentioned in these quotidian passages is that Elizabeth Ayers, at the time she recorded these thoughts, was already a Civil War widow. The man she was soon to marry, Daniel T. Martin, a veteran of the Kansas Fifth Volunteers, had helped bury her husband, Cpl. Benjamin Franklin Ayers, during the very month that Elizabeth turned twenty-three. Elizabeth herself died at age forty-three.

Life on the American frontier could be hard and lonely, but sewing and quiltmaking often provided warmth in more than the obvious ways. "For the winter I think I shall make a quilt to keep from getting lonesome," a woman from Minnesota wrote to a friend.

To survive the solitude, friends and relatives in distant locales sometimes enclosed in their letters swatches of cloth from quilts or dresses they were making as a tactile reminder of themselves. These bits of shared material were often saved as a keepsake or incorporated into a quilt. "My treasure box" is the childhood name Lois Lenski had for the box of scraps she saved from her mother's sewing. In such ways, cloth came to be indelibly imprinted with comforting references, and the quilts made from these pieces of cloth became potent reminders of loved ones.

There was also a social side to quiltmaking. Working side by side over a quilt gave women a welcome opportunity to talk and share their lives. Lizzie Fant Brown, a former slave who lived and reared eight children in rural Mississippi, remembers "big times at the quiltings and big eatin' afterwards." (Brown's life story was recorded by a WPA interviewer when she was seventy-six years old.)

While sewing was sometimes a social event, more often it was a solitary, repetitive activity, a necessary task in order to clothe one's family at a time when store-bought goods were still a luxury. "I am weary," Ruth Anna Abrams, an Indiana housewife, confesses to her diary in 1881. "I have sewed hard all day."

She had reason to feel tired. Abrams bore a total of nine children, the last delivered at home late in the year she was writing, with only her husband at hand to help—"a hard man to keep in good humor," she wrote of him privately. How she found time to keep a journal at all is a wonder. And yet she found it in herself, like many of these women, to collect her thoughts and mark the passage of time with a diary.

My grandmothers, mother, and aunts saved letters to and from parents, husbands during the war, children away visiting relatives or at church camp, as well as greeting cards, school projects, travel souvenirs, and report cards, among many other things—all the small and seemingly insignificant objects that mark the fact that we were here; we spent time on this earth; we were a family; we mattered.

I have often wondered whether this habit of gathering up, saving and refusing to throw things away, is a Midwestern trait. It certainly filled cedar chests, desk drawers, and boxes high atop closet shelves in my Midwestern family home. Even today when I visit, I'll pull down a box just to look through it.

As Lydia Marie Child's oft-quoted lines from *The American Frugal Housewife* noted, "Nothing should be thrown away so long as it is possible to make any use of it." I agree with both the practical sentiment of Child's line and its deeper meaning: that by gathering up the tiny fragments, nothing precious shall be lost.

private
thoughts

Chronicles charting the progress of home-sewing projects crop up frequently in diaries and letters, a reflection perhaps of their importance in the writer's life, or simply of the sheer number of hours these projects required. The steady and painstaking process of assembling and finishing a quilt was evidently worth keeping track of.

Diaries and oral histories of the period make note of needlework projects in a most unself-consciousness way. The women of the day weren't speaking to posterity; they were simply marking their place on the everyday timeline, when life and meaningful work were largely one and the same.

Yet quilts, like diaries, are an accumulation of bits and pieces of the maker's life, a repository of ideas, hopes, and feelings. Today, examining a quilt brings to mind many questions about the maker and what she was thinking as she worked. For the most part, those thoughts will remain locked inside the precise, regular stitches.

14. Friday

Didn't get up very early. had
the toothache worked pretty
busy most all day In the afternoon
went down town and brought 17 yd
of cotton cloth, costing in all, $5.70
Run around a little in the evening
Wrote a letter to W F M

Sewed and crocheted and made tatting. Don't feel very happy...finished fixing my quilt.... 111th boys came home last night. [The 111th Ohio Volunteer Infantry Regiment was organized in Toledo in 1862.]

WEDNESDAY, JULY 19

Wrote a letter in the morning to D.T.M. [Daniel Thomas Martin, her fiancé] then went to quilting and quilted all day in the eve got a letter from D.T.M. thought it not a very good letter and had a notion to write a saucy answer but concluded not to....

WEDNESDAY, AUG 16

Got some help on my quilt. Had a real good time.... Got two dear good letters from Mr. M. [fiancé].

TUESDAY, AUGUST 22

As usual done up the morning's work. Afterward went to my quilt and worked on it until it got so dark I couldn't see anymore. Nothing of importance transpired that I am aware of.

WEDNESDAY, AUG 23

Quilted steady all forenoon got my quilt off a little after noon then bound it which took me till bedtime....

FRIDAY, SEPT. 15

My birthday, 25 years old....

Diary of ELIZABETH HOSACK AYERS MARTIN,
Ohio, 1865

LEFT, *FROG IN THE POND*, C.1860–1880, PENNSYLVANIA.
RIGHT, WOOD NEEDLE CASE, C. 1880, TIROL.

You may be sure that any chance scrap of chintz, gingham, or calico once gay, now, it may be faded by time, wear, and frequent washings, may bring to her mind as many tender memories as are recalled to another by the dried rose, the sprig of forget-me-not, or the true lover's knot put away with tender care in some private drawer.

SCRIBNER'S *magazine, 1894*

I have done quite a lot of canning of what is left of our fruit and vegetables and for the winter I think I shall make a quilt to keep from getting lonesome, for some of the women around here are real interested in quilting again.

A Minnesota woman writing to a friend in 1931

OPPOSITE, *FLYING GEESE,* C. 1825–1850, PENNSYLVANIA.
ABOVE, *POSTAGE STAMP STAR,* 1880–1900, PENNSYLVANIA.
THE QUILTING BEE, FRANK UTPATEL, WPA WOOD ENGRAVING.

I wish I was one of those sassy sorts that never gets in a fret over anything. Didn't this sewing machine help me along fast. I never mean to sew by hand any more if I can help it.

Letter to Anne Whitwell from her daughter in March 1867

VARIABLE STAR, 1870–1880, PENNSYLVANIA;
ADVERTISING TRADE CARDS.

apron

apron

cravat

bonnet Ribons   1846, Emmel & Goi

Fri. 1st,   sewed.

Sat. 2nd. ———   sewed. eve. at singing

Sun 3d. Pa, Ma and Sat. Johns Holdermans

Mon. 4th. Washed. Cal. started to school.

Tues. 5th. ironed. sewed. Miss ~~Sara Ann~~ Rovere was

Wed. 6th. sewed.

JULY [1895]

31st Wed.   Put my charm quilt in the frame   quilted

AUG

9th Fri.   churned   finished my quilt, After
    supper I went to see G. Hann's baby it is very
    sick with cholera

SEPT.

9th Mon. washed   pieced quilt
16th Mon. washed   P.M. cut out 9 calico dresses

SEPTEMBER [1896]

Tues 1st   quilt[ed]   finished 3 P.M.
Tues 8th   ironed   quilted   pealed peaches
Wed 9th   canned peaches
Thurs 10th   went to town had a tooth pulled. got a
    calico dress P.M.   quilted.   Emma Overhalt died
    in morn.

ABOVE, STERLING
SILVER THIMBLE
CASE, TIFFANY &
CO., EARLY 20TH
CENTURY, UNITED
STATES. OPPOSITE,
A PAGE FROM ELIZA
TILLINGHAST'S
19TH-CENTURY
FABRIC DIARY.

Diary of an unknown writer in Indiana, from 1895–1902

17

Mabel had a fine rag doll with a bisque head and many fine clothes which had belonged to our great-grandmother. Dolls did not, however, particularly appeal to me. Once I was given a cloth doll with a china head, but she did not last long. I took her down to the corral to watch the cowboys brand calves, and she got excited and fell off the fence and broke her head.

EDITH STRATTON KITT,
writing later in her life about growing up in Arizona in the 1880s

ABOVE, "INDIA," CHINA DOLL, C. 1865, EUROPE. RIGHT AND OPPOSITE, ADVERTISING TRADE CARDS, C. 1890.

JAN 17 SAT [1914]

*Babe & I spent the day with Aunt Susan,
started silk quilt.*

FEB 28 SAT

*Our 2nd aniversary. Not a word from Harold.
It surely means nothing to him. I am sorry we
couldn't be together, we never can be tho if he
doesn't save his money and learn how to trust a
wife. Aunt Susan was here by surprise and
started to set worsted quilts together.
Babe can roll over.*

Diary of EDITH LISLE PEMBLE, *Linden, Iowa*

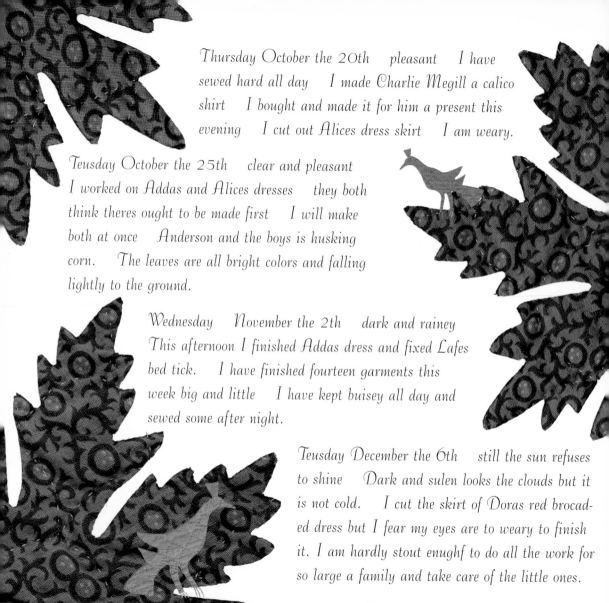

Thursday October the 20th   pleasant   I have sewed hard all day   I made Charlie Megill a calico shirt   I bought and made it for him a present this evening   I cut out Alices dress skirt   I am weary.

Teusday October the 25th   clear and pleasant I worked on Addas and Alices dresses   they both think theres ought to be made first   I will make both at once   Anderson and the boys is husking corn.   The leaves are all bright colors and falling lightly to the ground.

Wednesday   November the 2th   dark and rainey This afternoon I finished Addas dress and fixed Lafes bed tick.   I have finished fourteen garments this week big and little   I have kept buisey all day and sewed some after night.

Teusday December the 6th   still the sun refuses to shine   Dark and sulen looks the clouds but it is not cold.   I cut the skirt of Doras red brocaded dress but I fear my eyes are to weary to finish it. I am hardly stout enughf to do all the work for so large a family and take care of the little ones.

Diary of RUTH ANNA ABRAMS, *Indiana, 1881.*
A mother of nine children, she died in 1883 at age forty-two.

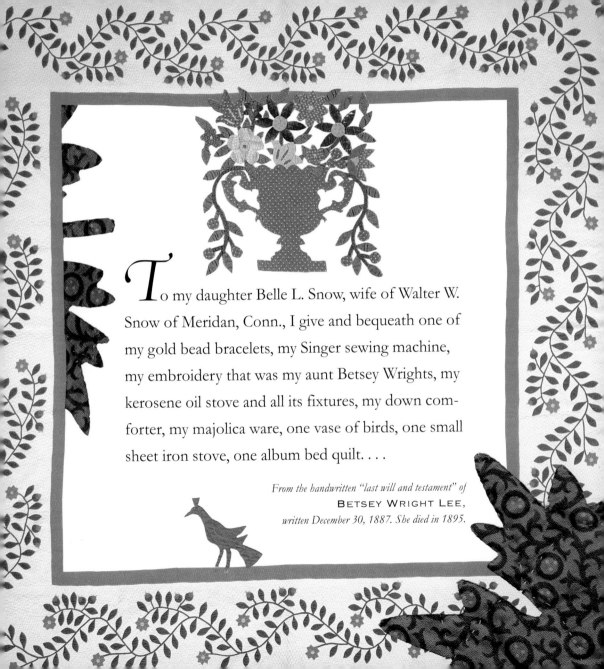

*T*o my daughter Belle L. Snow, wife of Walter W. Snow of Meridan, Conn., I give and bequeath one of my gold bead bracelets, my Singer sewing machine, my embroidery that was my aunt Betsey Wrights, my kerosene oil stove and all its fixtures, my down comforter, my majolica ware, one vase of birds, one small sheet iron stove, one album bed quilt. . . .

From the handwritten "last will and testament" of
BETSEY WRIGHT LEE,
written December 30, 1887. She died in 1895.

Family
&
Friends

The years when quiltmaking came into full flower—from the 1820s to the 1880s—were a time of large-scale migration in America.

Taking their quilts with them (often gifts from family members who remained behind), women left comfortable homes in New England and on the Atlantic seaboard, heading for the wilds of Wisconsin, Mississippi, or Kentucky. Later they would watch as the daughters and granddaughters whom they had taught to sew pressed onward to Texas, Oregon, or California.

Just as quilting parties brightened a pioneer woman's social circle, the quilts themselves—sometimes even mere swatches of cloth tucked into a letter—became talismans of old friends and loved ones who were far away.

Those quilts and personal memoirs that survive provide eloquent testimony of love and affection, still being stitched into quilts today.

Tuesday, Dec. 4 [1827]

Engaged in making my little boy's clothes all day, while he by my side reading or playing, has been my comfort and delight.

From a letter written by
MRS. LOUISA HIGGINSON,
mother of ten, Cambridge, Massachusetts

I have been looking for something to send
to you, but I could not find anything that I
could send in a letter bitt a piece of my
new dress. . . .

HANNAH SHAW, *1850, Wisconsin, from a letter to her daughter, Margaret*

OPPOSITE, *ALPHABET*, C. 1940–1950, NORTH CAROLINA; ADVERTISING
TRADE CARD. ABOVE, ELIZA TILLINGHAST'S 19TH-CENTURY FABRIC DIARY.

*E*very young girl should piece one quilt at least to carry away with her to her husband's home, and if her lot happens to be cast among strangers, as is often the case, the quilt when she unfolds it will seem like the face of a familiar friend, and will bring up a whole host of memories, of mother, sister, friend, too sacred for us to intrude upon.

GOOD HOUSEKEEPING,
April 14, 1888

ABOVE, DETAIL FROM *ALBUM*, 1873, FOUND IN IOWA. **INSET RIGHT,** *ROAD TO CALIFORNIA*, BEGUN 1859, FINISHED 1884. **RIGHT,** *TRIPLE IRISH CHAIN*, 1898, OHIO; ADVERTISING TRADE CARD. C. 1887.

*W*hen I was eleven,
[Grandma] encour-
aged me to piece a quilt. She helped
me cut the pieces and showed me
how to join the blocks together. It
was the Irish chain pattern. I worked willingly
at first for I liked to sew, and then I bogged
down. I had not yet learned the discipline of
carrying a task through to the end, so Grandma
came to my rescue. The quilt would never have
been finished without her help. I
kept it all through my married life,
a remembrance of her.

LOIS LENSKI'S *memoir,*
c. 1904, Anna, Ohio

*M*other always bought needles and thread and dry goods, and put them to good use making clothes for the family, and teaching my sister and me to sew. Before I was five years old I had pieced one side of a quilt, sitting at her knee half an hour a day, and you may be sure she insisted on tiny stitches.

EDITH WHITE'S
*remembrances of
her childhood in
the 1860s in
French Corral,
California,
from her 1936
memoir*

LEFT, 19TH-CENTURY
THREAD BOX. **OPPOSITE,**
ADVERTISING TRADE CARD,
C. 1890; DETAILS FROM A
1884–1890 CRAZY QUILT.

*M*ama made me get my crazy quilt out and embroider on it all morning because she wanted to keep me busy and it was all that I could do.

Diary of HALLIE RIDDLE, *Birmingham, Alabama, 1887*

All that we
could get to live in was a shabby old cabin
that a miner moved out of that we might
move in. Father and Mother cleaned it
up, and added to it. Then Father,
who didn't have any money to
buy furniture, made chairs and
tables out of drygoods boxes,
and Mother covered them with
chintz calico.

Years later Father used to say,
"That little cabin was the prettiest home
we ever had!" Some time afterwards
Father bought a frame house under a big
pine-tree, and we moved to it. Mother
planted flowers and father started an
orchard, and we had a fine vegetable garden. But we children liked best of all the
tall pine-tree. . . .

EDITH WHITE *from her 1936 memoir*

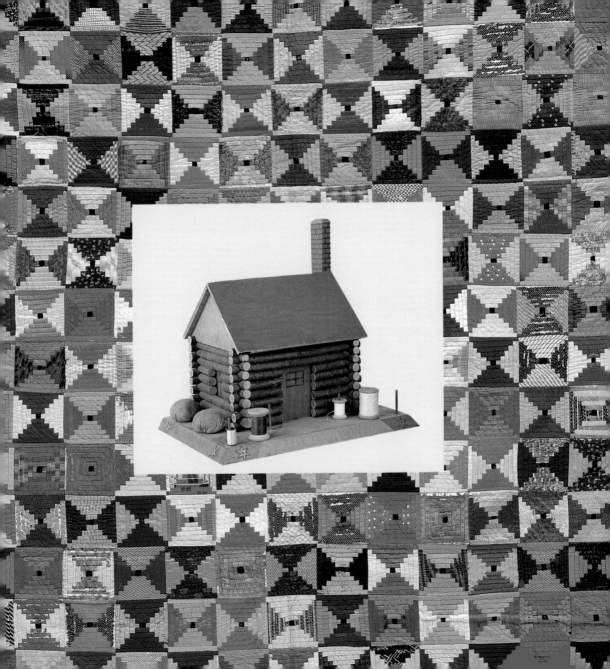

$\mathcal{M}$y father would take this scrap cotton to the mill and have it ginned, and he'd give my mother the cotton, and she'd get this ticking and make a new mattress and fill it fulla this fresh cotton. She'd make one or two new mattresses each year, and we had pillows outa cotton just like that, and my mother would always make quilts—she'd pad them with scrap cotton. We had plenty quilts and we stayed *warm*.

SARA BROOKS'S *memories of growing up in Alabama in the early 1900s*

LEFT, DETAIL OF *BLOCKS*, C. 1870–1890, NEW YORK STATE. ABOVE, DETAIL FROM *ALBUM*, 1873, FOUND IN IOWA. RIGHT, *CABIN IN THE COTTONS III*, HORACE PIPPIN, 1944.

FEATHERED STAR, 1840–1860,
OHIO; IVORY NEEDLE CASE,
C. 1790, THE NETHERLANDS.
OPPOSITE, *BRICK WALL*,
C. 1890–1910.

Blankets, and bed-quilts and bed-comforters, where persons are still unwise enough to use the quilts and comforters, instead of the more healthful blankets, should be sent to the wash-tubs at once, whether they seem to be soiled or not. If they have been used, they have taken upon themselves the exhalations of the human bodies that have slept under them, and they need the purification of soap, water, and sunlight.

PETERSON MAGAZINE, *November 1876*

Comfortables—to renovate. After washing and thoroughly drying bed-quilts, fold and roll them tight, then give them a beating with the rolling-pin to liven up the batting, and make them soft and new.

From the UNIVERSAL HOUSEHOLD ASSISTANT, OR
WHAT EVERY ONE SHOULD KNOW:
A CYCLOPEDIA OF PRACTICAL INFORMATION

Emory Chapel

$\mathcal{F}$eb 19, 1903. Presented Mrs. Lily Davis a comfort as a token of appreciation for serving as janitor of church.

From the LADIES AID SOCIETY
ledger book, West Millgrove, Ohio

LEFT, CRAZY, c. 1910–1935;
DETAIL OF EMORY CHAPEL,
1896, NEW YORK. **ABOVE
AND RIGHT, 19TH-CENTURY
PIECED BLOCKS.**

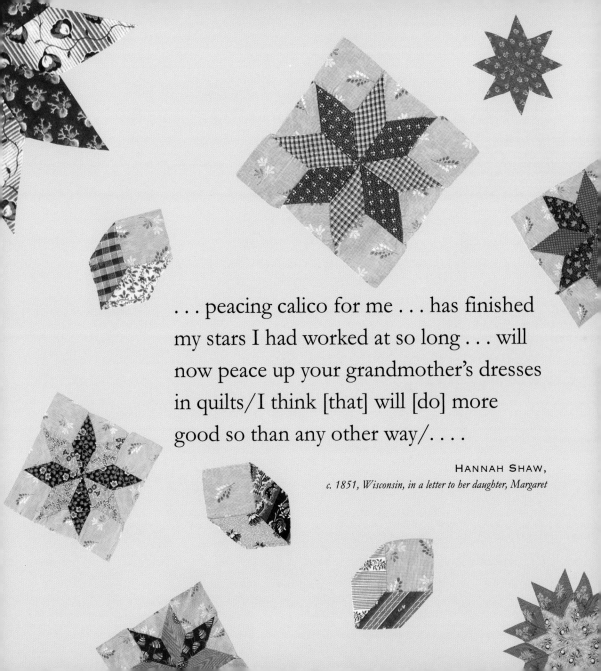

. . . peacing calico for me . . . has finished
my stars I had worked at so long . . . will
now peace up your grandmother's dresses
in quilts/I think [that] will [do] more
good so than any other way/. . . .

HANNAH SHAW,
c. 1851, Wisconsin, in a letter to her daughter, Margaret

NINE PATCH, C. 1870–1880. **INSET**, *LYNCHBURG NEGRO DANCE*, FROM THE
LEWIS MILLER SKETCHBOOK, 1853.

We had big times at the quiltings and big eatin' afterwards. They would make two quilts a night and they were nice quilts too with hems and everything. The Nine Patch pattern was a beauty, with little squares no bigger than your thumb nail.

From an interview with LIZZIE FANT BROWN
at age seventy-six, Mississippi

domestic

economy

*N*ineteenth-century women prided themselves on being frugal, practical people. Women served as keepers of the household ledgers, and these record books show that every yard of thread and calico was accounted for as carefully as flour, sugar, and other staples. Even after the advent of inexpensive, machine-made cottons, quilters often reused pieces of their favorite fabrics.

If women were meticulous in making use of their materials, they were even more so when it came to budgeting their time. Striking a balance between the practical and the artistic was an ongoing struggle, and if a task could encompass both, so much the better. In the garden, rows were arranged with a pleasing sense of order, purpose, and beauty. And so were their quilts. Was this unconscious behavior, or simply an unspoken pact among women, individually and collectively, to find a way within their household domains, to express themselves on deeper, more creative levels?

This is the last day of Nov. I ordered meat & bread of central meat market got dinner and I did the work and did sewing all the afternoon mended some of my cloth ing in the forenoon and did some other work and spent most of the afternoon on the quilt I am making I have not ironed the washing I did. . . . I have 64 blocks pieced and in a box upstairs on my table at east side or head corner of my bed

Diary of MRS. EMMA J. KORNS, *Grinnell, Iowa*

To make a silk quilt—This is a light and convenient article for a couch or for a child's crib, and will be found extremely useful in a sick-room. It can be made very economically out of two silk dresses, after the bodies are past wear. . . .

From MISS LESLIE'S LADY'S HOUSE-BOOK:
A MANUAL OF DOMESTIC ECONOMY

LEFT, *WILD GOOSE CHASE,* C. 1835–1855, MASSACHUSETTS. RIGHT, TINTYPE, TWO UNKNOWN WOMEN, LATE 19TH CENTURY.

I 'member de firs' dollar I ever made. . . . I tuk dat dollar an' bot me some calico an' made me sum Quilts; I wuz so proud to have my own quilts an' pillows an' things."

From an interview with JANE MCLEOD WILBURN
at age eighty-seven, Mississippi

Monday. worked muslin most all day, dancing school public this evening did not attend. finished my muslin borders.

Diary of **MARY B. HODGE**
*of Buffalo, New York,
during a visit to Toledo, Ohio*

OPPOSITE, *DOUBLE WEDDING RING,* C.
1935–1945, ARKANSAS; DETAIL FROM ALBUM,
1873. **RIGHT,** THIMBLE, SIMONS, APPLIED GRAPES,
PAT. 1907; ALBUM, C. 1850, NEW ENGLAND.

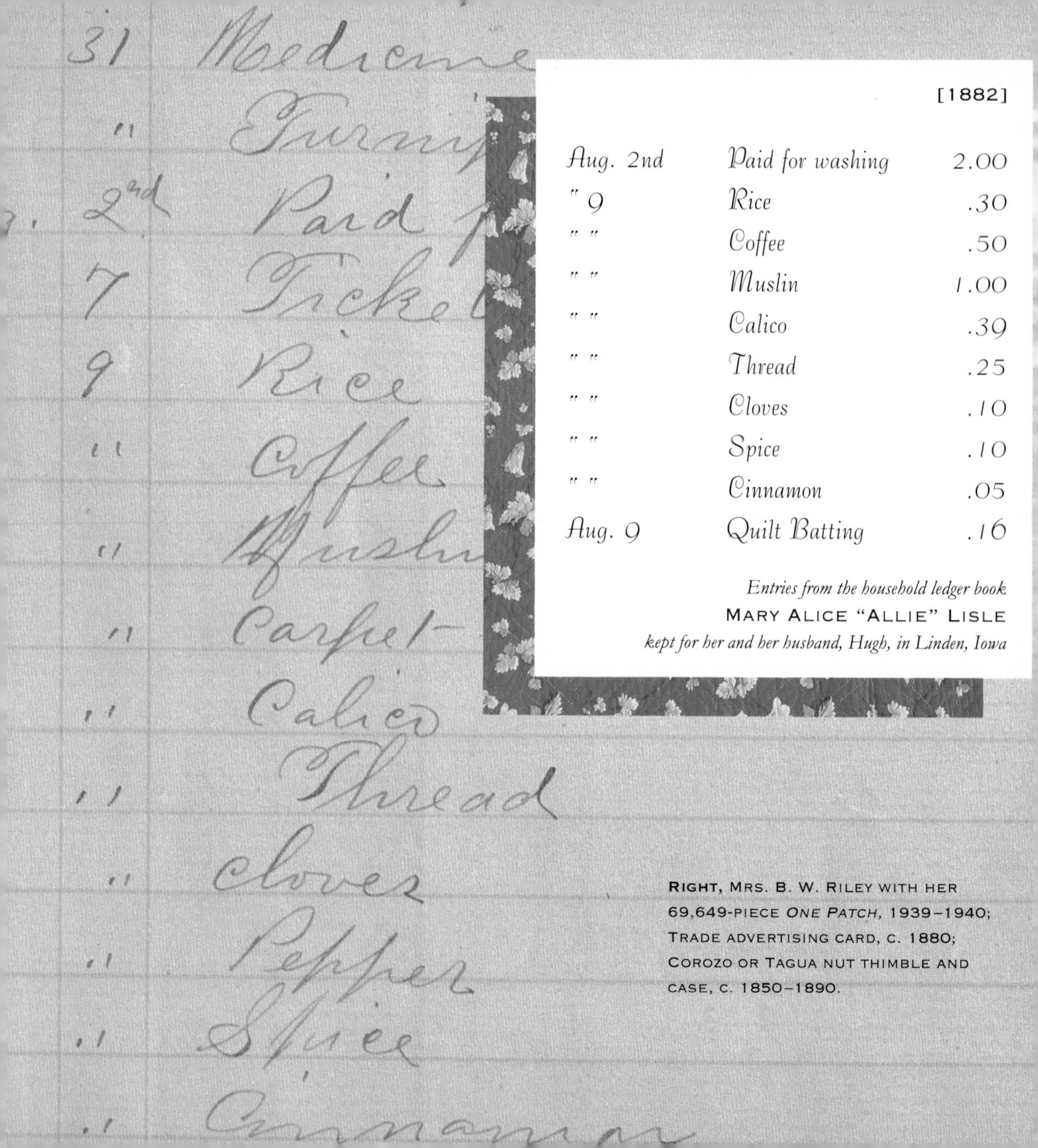

Handwritten ledger (left)

31	Medicine
"	Turnip
2nd	Paid
7	Ticket
9	Rice
"	Coffee
"	Muslin
"	Carpet—
"	Calico
"	Thread
"	Cloves
"	Pepper
"	Spice
"	Cinnamon

Printed transcription box

[1882]

Aug. 2nd	Paid for washing	2.00
" 9	Rice	.30
" "	Coffee	.50
" "	Muslin	1.00
" "	Calico	.39
" "	Thread	.25
" "	Cloves	.10
" "	Spice	.10
" "	Cinnamon	.05
Aug. 9	Quilt Batting	.16

Entries from the household ledger book
MARY ALICE "ALLIE" LISLE
kept for her and her husband, Hugh, in Linden, Iowa

RIGHT, MRS. B. W. RILEY WITH HER
69,649-PIECE *ONE PATCH*, 1939–1940;
TRADE ADVERTISING CARD, C. 1880;
COROZO OR TAGUA NUT THIMBLE AND
CASE, C. 1850–1890.

Mrs B W Riley

*T*his quilt contains 62,948 separate pieces. It is the work of Mrs. M. A. Haggard of White Cloud, Kansas. She commenced it in 1895 at 80 years of age, completed in 2 years. It took 36 yards of cloth and 24 spools of thread to make it. . . .

Inscription stamped on the back of MARTHA HAGGARD'S *1897 quilt*

ABOVE, BRASS AND
STEEL BIRD SEWING
CLAMP, PAT. 1853,
UNITED STATES.
RIGHT, VARIABLE
STAR, C. 1830–1855,
PENNSYLVANIA;
ADVERTISING TRADE
CARD, C. 1890.

48

QUILTING WITH CLARK'S O.N.T.

*T*he decree has gone forth that a revival of patchwork quilts is at hand, and dainty fingers whose owners have known only patches and patchwork from family description are busy placing the blocks together in new and artistic patterns, as well as in the real old-time order.

THE LADIES' HOME JOURNAL, *October 1894*

ABOVE, STEEL BIRD SEWING CLAMP, C. 1830, UNITED STATES. LEFT, ADVERTISING TRADE CARD, C. 1890.

I began to sew for my dolls when I was six. Mama showed me how to cut a pattern, set in sleeves, how to gather a skirt to put it in a belt, how to make button-holes, how to do hemstitch-ing. She said, "If you are going to learn to sew, you might as well do it the right way." The box of scraps from her own dressmaking was my treasure box.

From LOIS LENSKI'S *autobiography*

THE FIRST LESSON

I was permitted to have material
with which I cut out, fitted, and
made on the sewing machine a dress
for my sister when I was eleven. Of
this I was justly proud.

EDITH WHITE

*T*he true economy
of housekeeping is simply the art
of gathering up
all the fragments, so
that nothing be lost.
I mean the fragments
of *time,* as well as
materials. Nothing
should be thrown
away so long as it is
possible to make any
use of it, however
trifling that use may be....

LYDIA MARIE CHILD,
The American Frugal Housewife, 1832

LEFT AND OPPOSITE, *ELONGATED NINE PATCH,*
1870–1890. ABOVE, DETAIL FROM AN 1885 CRAZY QUILT.
RIGHT, THE HIRAM HOUSE SOCIAL SETTLEMENT;
ADVERTISING TRADE CARD, C. 1900; HELEN GREEN'S
HOUSEHOLD ACCOUNT BOOK, APRIL 22, 1880.

Commenced housekeeping
April 22nd 1880.

Accounts commencing
April 28th 1880.
Freight on furniture 1.20
" Coffee $1.00
" Sundries 1.02
" Book .25
21st " [...]

G. W. Newman & Co.,   Emporia, Kansas.

WARRANTY   UNLIMITED

" Mending Coffee pot .10
" Ammonia .10
" Condition powder caps .60
" Lumber $1.20
" Mending Waggon $7.20
"   Hat .35
7th Codfish .30
"   Hat .25
" Alum & Borax .11
" Frying pan .70

Apr. 15 - 1939.
   Mrs. Lely's Quilt. No. 3.
Batt   .40
Thread (2-300 yd) (1-192 yd)   .23
Muslin   .88
Postage   .02
Tax   .03
                            ¼ 1.55
Marking   2.
Quilting @ 4   7.82
Binding   .75
Postage   .17
                              12.39

         Paid in full

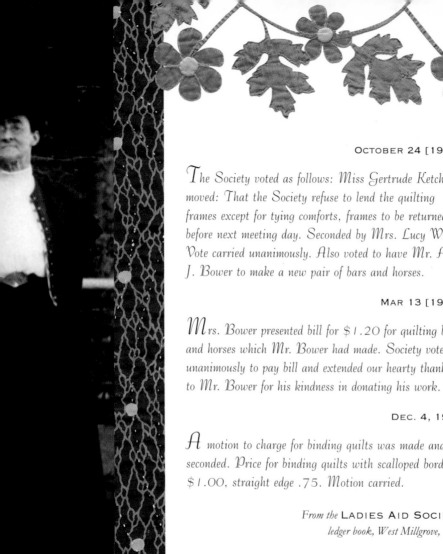

OCTOBER 24 [1928]

The Society voted as follows: Miss Gertrude Ketcham moved: That the Society refuse to lend the quilting frames except for tying comforts, frames to be returned before next meeting day. Seconded by Mrs. Lucy Wirt. Vote carried unanimously. Also voted to have Mr. A. J. Bower to make a new pair of bars and horses.

MAR 13 [1929]

Mrs. Bower presented bill for $1.20 for quilting bars and horses which Mr. Bower had made. Society voted unanimously to pay bill and extended our hearty thanks to Mr. Bower for his kindness in donating his work.

DEC. 4, 1930

A motion to charge for binding quilts was made and seconded. Price for binding quilts with scalloped border $1.00, straight edge .75. Motion carried.

From the LADIES AID SOCIETY
ledger book, West Millgrove, Ohio

LEFT, CORTE MADERA'S WOMEN'S IMPROVEMENT CLUB, c. 1908, CORTE MADERA, CALIFORNIA. INSET, AN ENTRY IN THE LEDGER BOOK OF THE LADIES AID SOCIETY OF WEST MILLGROVE, OHIO.

inscriptions
&
fancywork

Quiltmakers knew their work assumed a place in history, testifying to a needle-worker's skill and expertise.

Beyond their aesthetic value, however, quilts exist as a form of personal expression. They recall a brave, genuine, creative spirit. Those women who signed, initialed, or dated their work in thread left traces of themselves on the fabric. They might add an embroidered or inked inscription, often highly sentimental rhymes or moral precept, to express something of their intentions to us across the years.

Sometimes, however, quilt inscriptions served a more pragmatic purpose. Quiltmakers of every era have done their part to raise money for worthy causes. Women's societies frequently made quilts to be raffled, and selling squares of an album quilt, which were inscribed with the donor's names, was a popular fundraiser. Quilting was and continues to be women's way of making a valuable social contribution through their own handiwork.

IN MEMORY

OLIVE ELY

CHS

1926

As lonely through this world I stray,

And pass the pensive hours;

May truth and virtue point the way

And strewn my path with flowers.

M.E. Peach Maryland 1850

Quilt inscription

APPLIQUE, PROBABLY MADE IN THE SECOND
QUARTER OF THE 20TH CENTURY USING FABRICS
FROM THE MID-19TH CENTURY. **ABOVE,**
PAINTED SILK SEWING BOX, C. 1817,
PROBABLY NEW HAVEN, CONNECTICUT.

Sylvia Wall   Eugene   Mrs. A. Lorquin   Mrs. Fred Tombs.

Luella Douglas Ohio.   Mrs Frank J Gardner Chicago   Edgar J O Gardner   Grace T.

Mr John C Perry.   Mrs Lois A. Perry   Mr Chas. M. Dawson   Mrs Jennie L. Dawson

Charles Thiethethwaite Seattle   A. B. Wells   Henry Tozier.   Mrs Mar

Estelle.   Ralston Mc Cue   Geo. A. Burman.   Flora Mad. Graha

Wilbur Jackson.   Mrs Dollar   A M Henderson. Iowa.   Mr A L

Mrs M. H. Hammond   Emma M. Shaw.   Anna E Hammond   Mr Chas N. Rude

Adele Lorquin   Mrs Fannie Evans.   Mrs Isabel Greig.   Emily

M. C. Edwards.   Mrs. M. C. Edwards   Flora Gardiner   Mrs Parks.

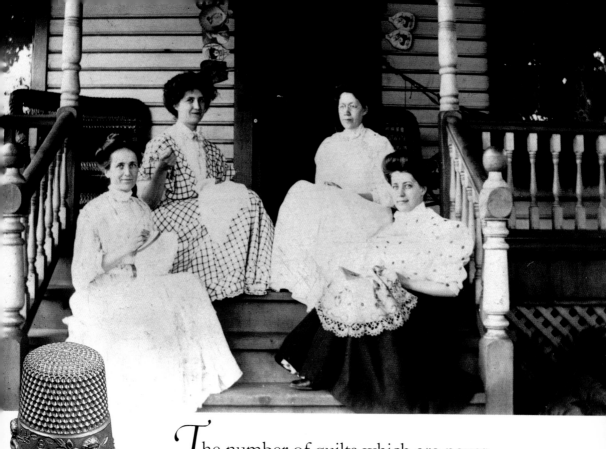

OPPOSITE, *BRICK WALL*
PRESENTATION QUILT, 1907,
CALIFORNIA. **ABOVE,** A
PHOTO OF WOMEN IN LODI,
OHIO, C. 1900; THIMBLE,
SIMONS, CUPID AND
GARLANDS, PAT. 1905.

$\mathcal{T}$he number of quilts which are never
used, but which are most carefully treasured by
their owners on account of some sentimental
or historic association, is far greater than
generally supposed.

From Marie D. Webster's 1915 book,
QUILTS: THEIR STORY AND HOW TO MAKE THEM

*A*fter 47 years of assiduous labor Mrs. S. Lizzie Weaves, a Bridgeton, N.J. woman, has just finished a crazy quilt of 30,075 patches.

KENT NEWS,
Chestertown, Maryland, January 4, 1890

PINWHEEL WITH *STREAK OF LIGHTNING* SASHING, C. 1880–1900, PENNSYLVANIA; SQUIRREL WOOD NEEDLE CASE, C. 1880, TIROL.

Dear old-fashioned quilts with your patches so gay,
You retain all the charm of an earlier day;
Like the old-fashioned garden our grandmothers grew,
Our love never wanes for them or you.
—Carlie Sexton

Log Cabin Barn Raising, 1930–1950, Indiana;
details from *Mariner's Compass*, c. 1840–1860.

Accept my friend this little pledge
Your love and friendship to engage
If ere we should be called to part
Let this be settled in your heart
That when this little peace you see
You ever will remember me
M.E.A.
Woodstock
1847

Inscription from quilt made by Betsey M. Wright;
detail from Album, 1873, found in Iowa